A Thousand Things Went Right Today!

Scrapbook Journal

This journal belongs to:

_____

_____

_____

by Ilan Shamir & Kris Baldwin

Published by Your True Nature, Inc
P.O. Box 272309
Fort Collins, CO 80527
email: grow@yourtruenature.com
800-992-4769

Visit our website at: www.yourtruenature.com

ISBN: 1-930175-09-4

Copyright 2002 YTN
A Thousand Things Went Right Today! is
a registered trademark of Your True Nature, Inc.

Thanks to the trees for their gift of paper!
Printed on Recycled Paper
We participate in the 100% Replanted program.
Tree seedlings have been planted in a protected watershed area
by the non-profit organization Trees, Water & People
for all paper used in the printing of this journal.
Visit http://www.ReplantTrees.org

Suggestions for using:

A
Thousand Things
Went Right Today!

Scrapbook Journal

Celebrate all the good each day! Gather pictures and write words to help remind you of all the things, large and small, that are going right in your life, and help keep your focus on all the good! There are places and spaces to record special people, special pets and even your gratitude! Use as a travel journal, grief journal or joy journal!

Sure it's so easy to let the things that aren't working take the drivers seat in our lives. Yet, we don't have to let the "glitches" run our day! Seeing the positive takes practice. It's like a muscle. The more you exercise it, the stronger it grows! Traveling through life with more joy and ease is absolutely possible. What you focus on grows and helps each day run smoother for you and those around you!

There are lots of wonderful ways to use this journal. Your way is the best way! Paste in pictures of special people, pets, favorite trees, flowers or special places that make a positive difference in your life . . . add images and words that inspire you and help you feel connected, relaxed and peaceful . . . paste in a leaf, write in a story . . . most of all have fun!

Yes, there are those days when you experience lifes' inevitable challenges seem overwhelming. Just picking up your journal filled with some of the good things in your life can be a wonderful comfort. And it can also help remind us that this too shall pass!

By focusing on what is working, each day becomes more of the smooth road you want and deserve! Travel on!

Ilan Shamir

Kris Baldwin

Contents

Celebrate... Life

Yourself

The World Around You

Even When Things Don't Go Right!

Special Places

Special People

Special Pets

Celebrate Gratitude!

"Life isn't about finding yourself.
Life is about creating yourself."
Gearge Bernard Shaw

Scrapbook Journal Tips

Put LIFE, FUN and CREATIVITY into your journal!

Use this as a guided journal or in any way you like such as for personal writing, travel or even recipes. There are many ways to journal or make scrapbook pages. Experiment and have fun! Your way is the BEST way!

Use colored pens or markers to write and draw fun squiggly lines and shapes. Include stickers or colored paper shapes.

Write around the perimeter of the photographs or objects you paste into this journal.

Unravel what holds you back... Release stress, blocks and negative emotions while shifting your focus back to the Thousands of Things That Are Going Right in YOUR Life!

Story of
A Thousand Things Went Right Today!

How many days have we let those little things or self doubt take a perfectly good day and turn it upside down? Within a fraction of a second, we've gone from pleasant thoughts, to pure agony, anger or frustration. A simple phone call, a jammed stapler, even a tiny accidental delete on the computer, shifts the focus, and all the good just seems to disappear. The downward spiral works at lightening speed as we are sucked into the abyss of EVERYTHING that has EVER gone wrong!

This is not where we enjoy living. We don't even enjoy visiting! Perhaps it's those old habits that started early. In school, a test would come back with five big red X's marking the wrong ones! If you ask me, I would have much rather had a nice blue check mark by the 95 ones I got right!

And there is this perfection thing! I don't know why we are so surprised when something does not go the way we would expect or prefer. Life does not always appear to be perfect. And yet, life's little glitches are just part of living. The desire to celebrate all the good in life, and help make this world better for all of us has inspired us to create and share *A Thousand Things Went Right Today* poem and journal.

Joy and living positively is our true nature. It is the way each day is meant to be lived in order to experience life fully! Maybe one day we will "*bump*" into each other and instead of saying *ouch*, we will say, "A Thousand Things Went Right Today!" *I met a new friend!*

A Thousand Things Went Right Today!

The Sun Came Up!
The Flowers Bloomed!
A Thousand Things Went Right Today!

My Elbow Bent
I Walked
I Breathed
Yes, A Thousand Things Went Right Today!

The Car Started and Hummed with Ease
The Door Opened Flawlessly
Sure, a Few Things Went Amiss, Awry
And Some Days More Than Others...
Yet, Thousands of Things are Going So Well...

The Birds Sang
A Friend Smiled
A Thousand Things Went Right Today!

I Am Grateful
My Life IS Working!
I Am So Grateful!
A Thousand Things Went Right Today!

They Went Right Yesterday...
And They Will Go Right Tomorrow!

Ilan Shamir

"Happiness is like jam.
You can't spread even a little,
without getting some on yourself."
Anonymous

People deal too much with the negative, or what is wrong . . .
Why not try and see positive things,
to just touch those things
and make them bloom."
Thich Nhat Hanh

Celebrate Life!

Even if we don't see the sun come up, it happens every day! So many things around us work and go right all the time! Sure there are little things that don't work, but who says they have to ruin a perfectly good day!

The alarm worked, the kids got off to school, we all arrived safely, I am alive, I helped others, I ate breakfast, I can listen, I went to work and I am grateful I have a job to go to. I am a good friend, I can get help when I need it, I can start fresh today . . . the list is endless!

Here is a place to reconnect and celebrate some of the simple ocurrences in life that are often overlooked. Each day is indeed an incredible gift!

Remember . . . stop and smell the roses . . . the daffodils . . . the petunias . . . the . . .

1.
2.
3.
4.
5.
6.
7.
8.
9.
10.
11.
12.
13.
14.
15.
16.
17.
18.
19.
20.
...
...
...

A Thousand Things Went Right Today!

"Keep your thoughts positive. Your thoughts become your words. Keep your words positive. Your words become your actions . . ."
Ghandi

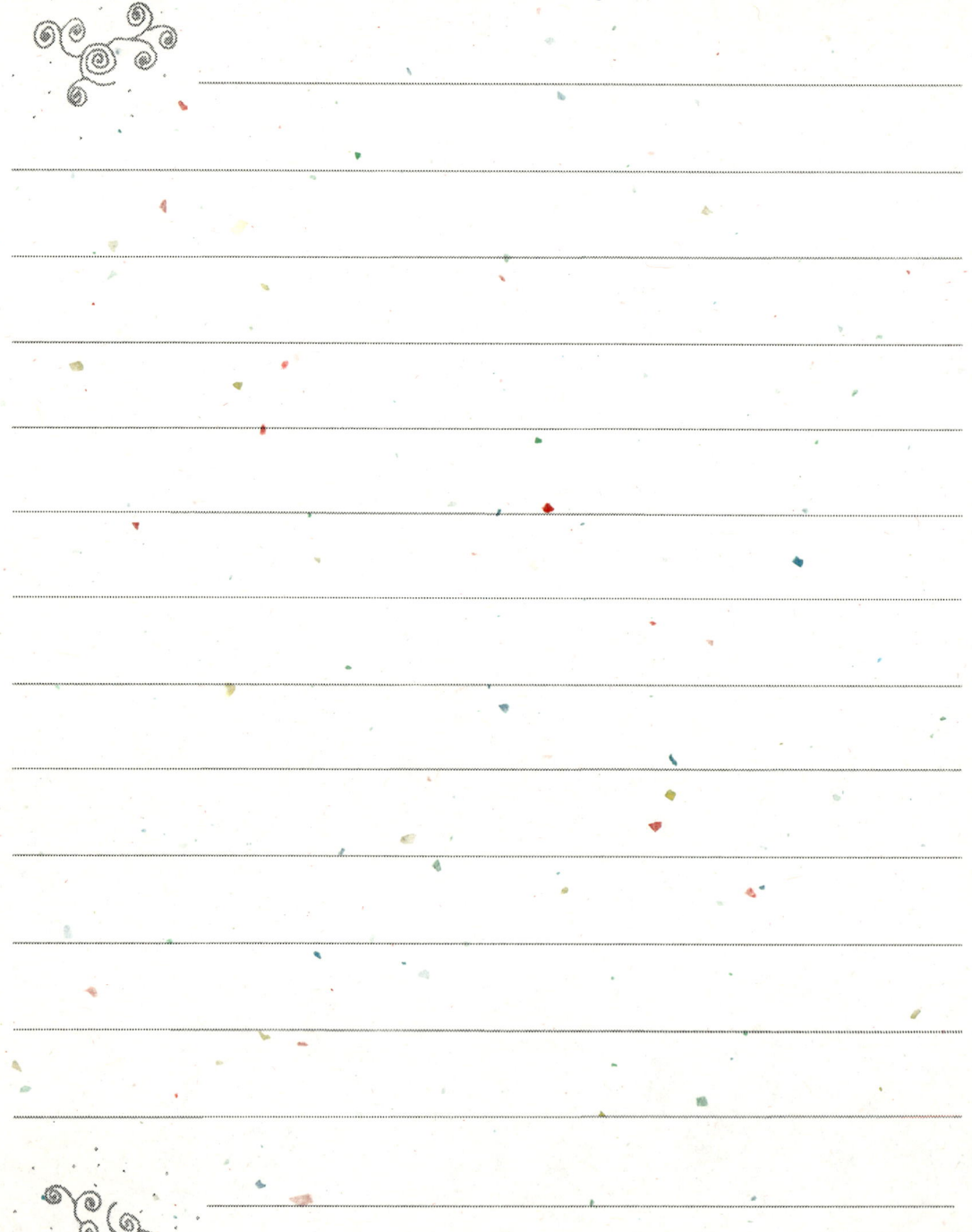

"Most folks are about as happy as they make their minds up to be!"
Abraham Lincoln

"Slow down and enjoy life.
It's not only the scenery you miss by going too fast...
you also miss the sense of where you are going, and why."
Eddie Cantor

"If you don't think every day is a great day try going without one."
Jim Evans

A Thousand Things Went Right Today!

"I have sometimes been wildly, despairingly, acutely miserable... but through it all I still know quite certainly that just to be alive is a grand thing."
Agatha Christie

Celebrate Yourself!

There are thousands of things to celebrate! Your talents, your qualities... your body... your uniqueness!

It's so easy to take our bodies for granted... they just keep doing so many things automatically without our having to think about it. That is until something goes wrong.

Sure there are some things that may not be working as we would like or are painful at times. We may even be sick or have physical disabilities. Yet there will ALWAYS be thousands of things that are working just fine. Celebrate and remember... thousands of things about you ARE absolutely perfect!

Things you feel are not working so well . . .

_____
_____
_____
_____

Ways to help yourself?

_____
_____
_____
_____
_____
_____
_____
_____
_____

Remember there are thousands of things that ARE going right with you EVERY moment !

1.
2.
3.
4.
5.
6.
7.
8.
9.
10.
11.
12.
13.
14.
15.
16.
17.
18.
19.
20.
...
...
...

A Thousand Things Went Right Today!

"Turn your face to the sunshine
and all shadows fall behind."
Helen Keller

> "What we do today, right now,
> will have an accumulated effect
> on all our tomorrows."
> Alexandra Stoddard

A Thousand Things Went Right Today!

1000+

A Thousand Things Went Right Today!

"When one door closes another one opens;
but we so often look so long, and
so regretfully upon the closed door,
that we do not see the ones which open for us."
Alexander Graham Bell

Celebrate the World Around You!

Sure there are things that break or the copier jams at work, yet there are SO MANY things that DO work each day! Every so often try to notice and mentally acknowledge everything when it does work. It's almost like a game... try it even for a few minutes and write down or sketch some of the things you notice are working around you. Breathe, smile, laugh, appreciate and delight in how more and more of the good seems to magically appear!

When you have this positive focus, the number of things that ARE working and going right will certainly outnumber the things that aren't going right.

1.
2.
3.
4.
5.
6.
7.
8.
9.
10.
11.
12.
13.
14.
15.
16.
17.
18.
19.
20.
...
...
...

A Thousand Things Went Right Today!

"The world we have created is a product of our thinking. It cannot be changed without changing our thinking."
Albert Einstein

*"Be the change
you want to see in the world."*
Gandhi

"Happiness depends upon ourselves."
Aristotle

A Thousand Things Went Right Today!

"I haven't failed,

I've found 10,000 ways that don't work."
Thomas Edison

Even when things don't go right... Celebrate!

How many days have we let the "little things" throw us off? Glitches seem to appear out of nowhere and totally catch us off guard! In a fraction of a second, the focus shifts from what is going right in the day, to everything that is going wrong. Stress, frustration and even anger flood in when we get a ticket or late fee, something is delayed or breaks, or when things do not unfold as we wanted them to happen...

And how long do we let these situations impact our day? The challenge is to remember to stop and take a deep breath, or get some fresh air and give the things that are not going right, only the amount of time and attention they deserve.

Keeping a sence of humor and focus on the positive things in life can't hurt! And remember...
there ARE thousands of things that are working in life EACH day!

What went wrong in your day?

_____
_____
_____
_____
_____
_____

Is there a bright side even to what went wrong?

_____
_____
_____
_____
_____
_____
_____
_____
_____
_____
_____

"In the middle of difficulty lies opportunity."
Albert Einstein

Remember Thousands of Things are going right all the while! . . .

1.
2.
3.
4.
5.
6.
7.
8.
9.
10.
11.
12.
13.
14.
15.
16.
17.
18.
19.
20.
...
...
...

A Thousand Things Went Right Today!

Some people call them "bumps" in the road of life,
rough spots... "glitches".
If a GLITCH was some sort of creature,
what it would look like?*

* If your Glitch is really big, you may want to find a counselor or someone to talk to...

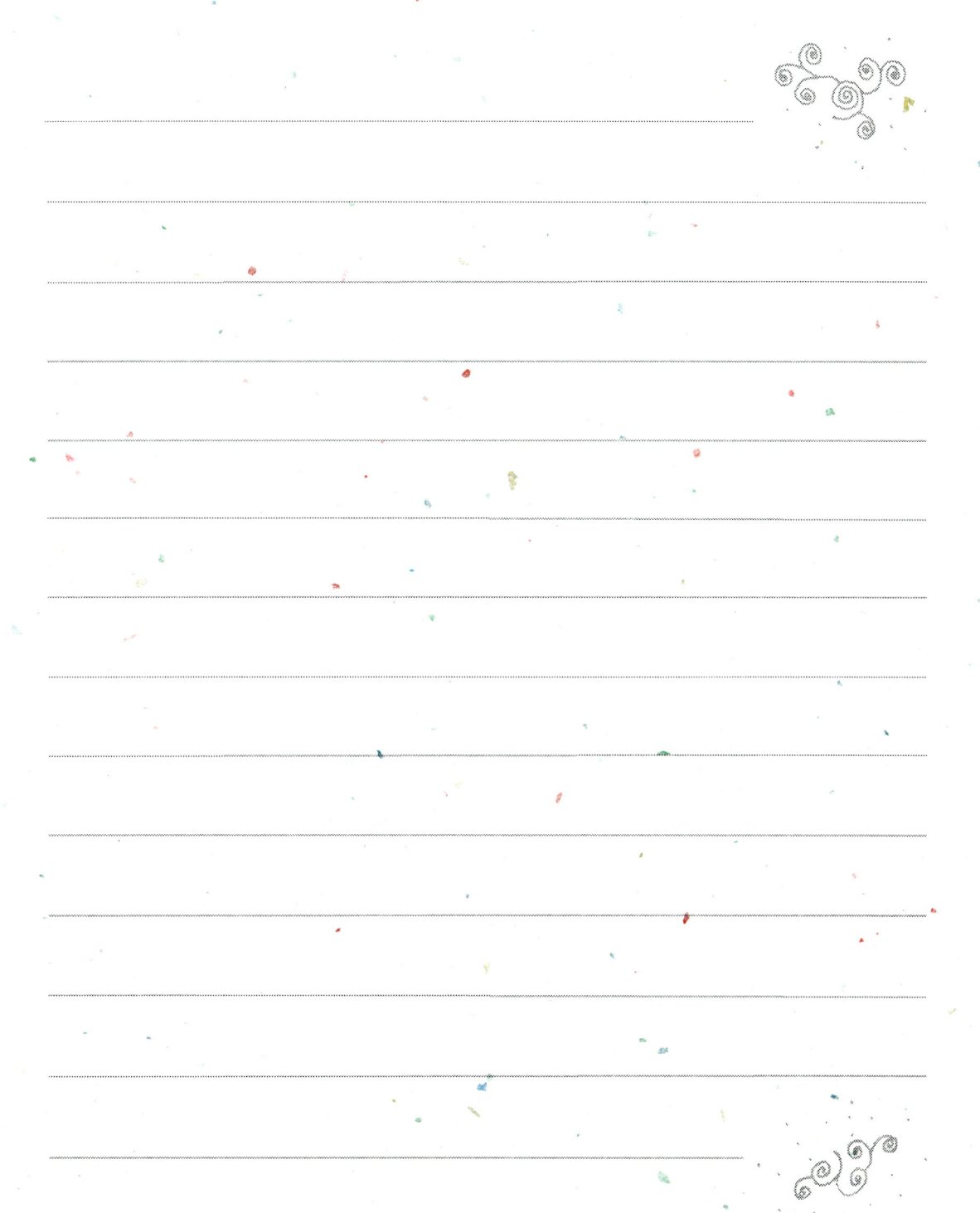

A Thousand Things Went Right Today!

Today I live in the quiet, joyous expectation of good.
Ernest Holmes

Celebrate Special Places!

We all have been to places where all of our stress melts away and we feel relaxed and peaceful. It may be a special treehouse you had when you were young, a walk in the woods or stroll along a favorite ocean beach. Perhaps it's just sitting under a tree or by a warm crackling fire.

The following pages have lots of space to paste, draw, doodle, write about, and dream about the WONDERFUL places you have been or would like to go that delight and refresh you!

"To affect the quality of the day;
that is the art of life."
Henry David Thoreau

> Life is a great big canvas,
> and you should throw
> all the paint
> you can on it!
> **Danny Kaye**

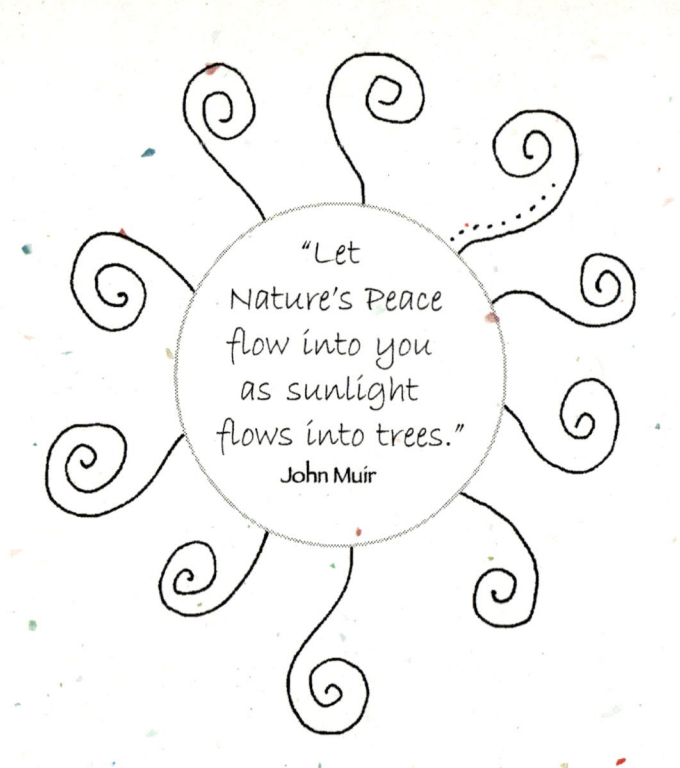

"Let Nature's Peace flow into you as sunlight flows into trees."
John Muir

"Keep your thoughts positive. Your thoughts become your words. Keep your words positive. Your words become your actions . . ."
Ghandi

1000+

A Thousand Things Went Right Today!

"A smile is a curve that sets everything straight."
Anonymous

Celebrate Special People!

Of the Thousands of things that go right each day, people are a big part of why things go right. Each of us is a special person! Have fun including things about the special people in your life.

Take some time and remember the people who have made a difference in your life and include pictures or write about special times you have shared together. Include family, friends, teachers and others, past or present that make a difference in your life!

"Let us be grateful to people who make us happy;
they are the charming gardeners who make our souls blossom."
Marcel Proust

"I don't make you feel special,
I just remind you
that you are special!"
David F. Sims

"We are, each of us angels
with only one wing;
and we can only fly
by embracing one another."

Luciano de Crescenzo

"We all live with the objective of being happy;
our lives are all different and yet the same."
Anne Frank

A Thousand Things Went Right Today!

"I want to sing like the birds sing
not worrying about who hears
or what they think."
Rumi

Celebrate Special Pets!

Animals are a wonderful source of unconditional love. No matter how smoothly each day goes, birds still sing and dogs can wag their tails to greet you! Animals have a special way of being able to cheer a person up!

Have fun remembering some of the pets you have known over the years. Or list the names of other people's pets you liked. Find or draw pictures about why they were special to you. Write about some of the special times you have shared.

"There is little that separates humans from other sentient beings — we all feel joy, we all deeply crave to be alive and to live freely, and we all share this planet together."

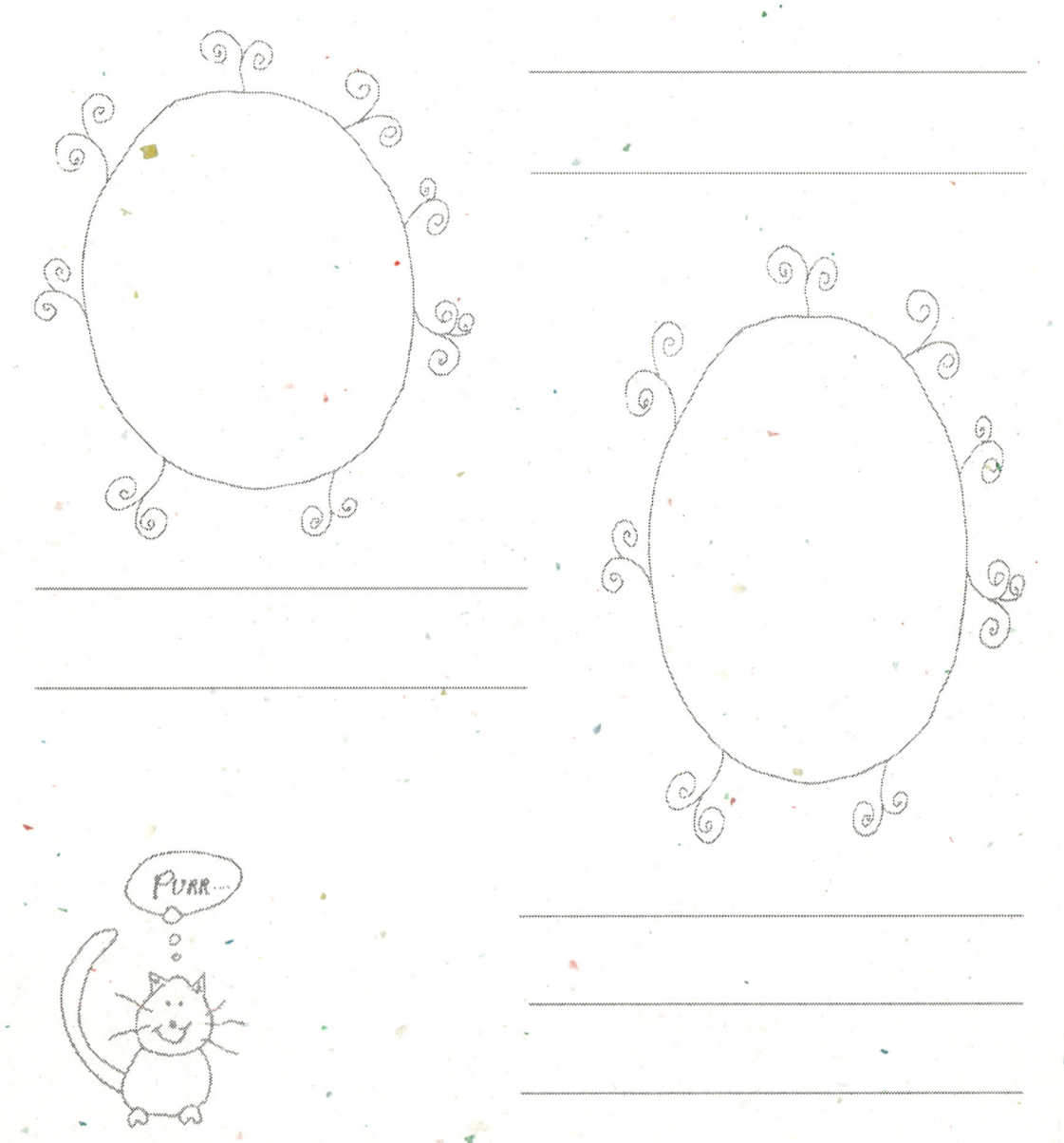

Gandhi

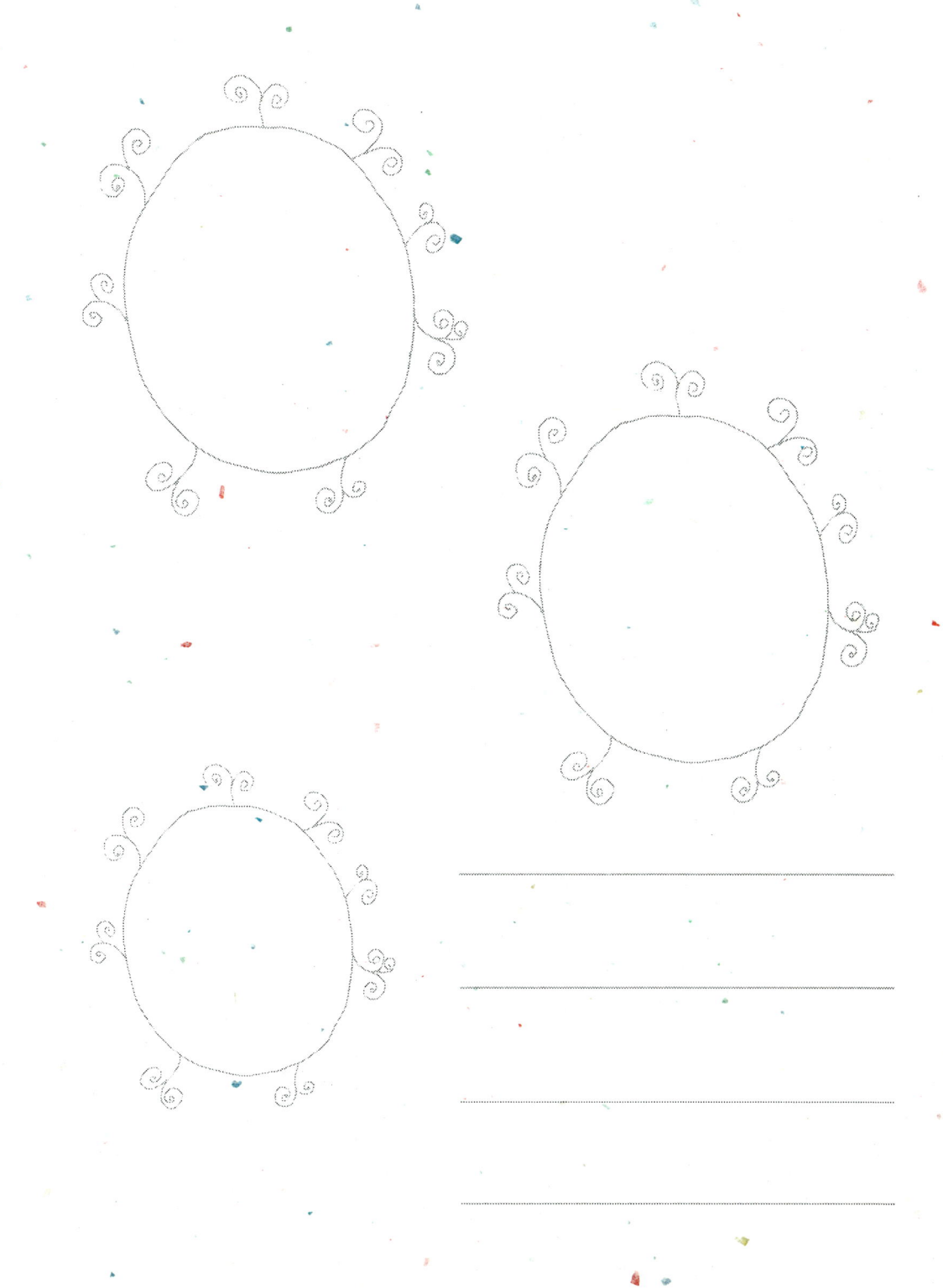

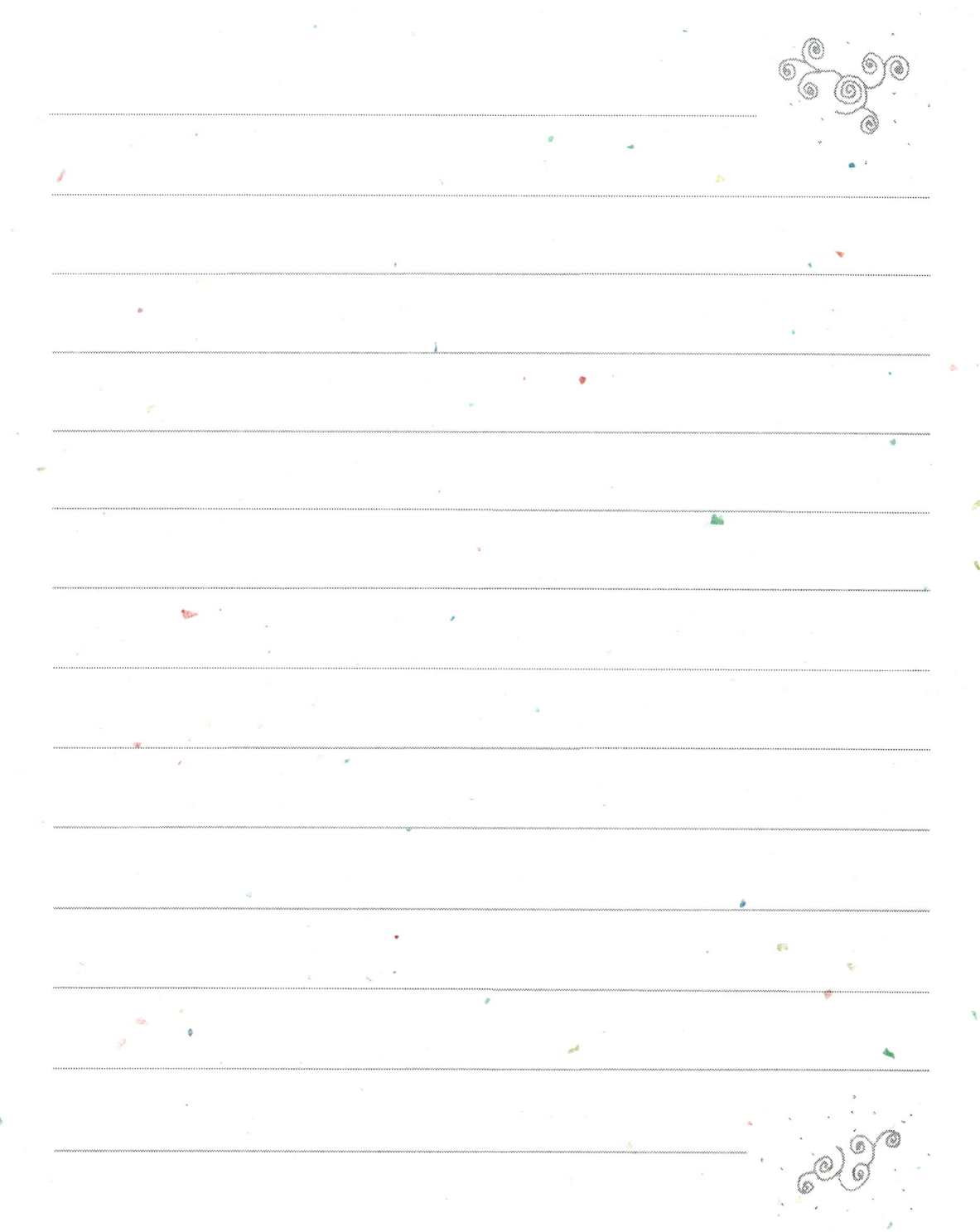

"The love for all living creatures is the noblest attribute of man."
Unknown

"It is man's sympathy with all creatures that first makes him truly a man."
Dr. Albert Schweitzer

1000+

A Thousand Things Went Right Today!

"Gratitude unlocks the fullness of life.
It turns what we have into enough, and more.
It turns denial into acceptance, chaos to order, confusion to clarity.
It can turn a meal into a feast, a house into a home,
a stranger into a friend.
Gratitude makes sense of our past, brings peace for today,
and creates a vision for tomorrow."
Melody Beattie

Celebrate Gratitude!

Thoughts and attitudes make a difference in our day! A Thousand Things Went Right Today! It is hard not to be grateful when you look at things this way...

Draw, write, paste pictures, cut out pictures from magazines, write a poem, tell a story about the thousands of things that you are grateful for!

"He is a wise man who does not grieve for the things which he has not, but rejoices for those which he has."

Epictetus

Gratitude is a Good Attitude!

I am grateful
for the overflowing
Beauty in Nature
Every Day!

So Many Things
Are Going Right
In My Life!

I am
Grateful!

"Develop an attitude of gratitude,
and give thanks for everything that happens to you, knowing that every step forward is a step toward achieving something bigger and better than your current situation."
Brian Tracy

1000+

A Thousand Things Went Right Today!

About the Authors

Ilan Shamir and Kris Baldwin live in Colorado, among the fluttering Aspen trees and breathtaking Rocky Mountains. "At Your True Nature, Inc. our love of trees and nature, inspires our art and our lives. We delight in creating products and programs that help make the world a better place for all of us!"

Ilan brings to life the wisdom, beauty and humor of human-nature through keynote performances, musical programs, and inspiring workshops. Kris expresses the beauty of nature through her laughter, smiles, love of gardening and pottery creations.

Advice from a Tree and *A Thousand Things Went Right Today* books, journals and gifts bring fun and celebration to life!

Your True Nature, Inc. has been featured in numerous magazine and television programs including The Wall Steet Journal, Good Housekeeping, Money Magazine, The London Times and National Public Radio-All Things Considered.

"Our true nature is to greet each day with joy and share our best gifts and talents!"

Visit us online at www.YourTrueNature.com

Imagine a world where the positive is celebrated more and more everyday. We invite you to share with us what went right in your day at home, at work, with your family . . . anywhere and anything!

Email us at: grow YourTrueNature.com visit our website www.YourTrueNature.com or send us a postcard or letter!

Also from Your True Nature

Books
Poet Tree-The Wilderness I Am
Tree Celebrations! - Ceremonies, Stories & Activities
Advice from a Tree®
A Thousand Things Went Right Today® - Mini GIFT Book

Journals
Advice from a Tree - Guided Journal
A Thousand Things Went Right Today® - Scrapbook Journal

Stationery
Notepads, Bookmarks, Postcards

Posters
Advice from a Tree®

Greeting Card and Gift in One!
Greeting Seeds, Greeting Teas, Greeting Scents,
Seasoned Greetings, Something Extra

Have a Tree Planted for Someone Special
For Birthday, Friendship, Memorial, Holidays

Keynotes, Programs and Workshops
Educational and inspiring programs in the areas of creativity, teamwork, nature, marketing and writing.

To order or book programs call 800-992-GROW(4769)
email: Grow@YourTrueNature.com
Website: www.YourTrueNature.com

Have a Tree Planted for Someone Special!

Your purchase price of $8.95 for one tree, or $18.95 for a three tree grove, plants and cares for this living gift in a protected watershed area by the non-profit organization Trees, Water and People. Native trees including Mahogany, Leucaena and Cedar will be planted for any occasion you choose. Here's the great part. The recipient not only gets a beautiful personalized greeting card from you, but both you and the recipient can visit the planting area online.

A simple, thoughtful and lasting gift.

It's as easy as 1, 2, TREE!

1. Use this order form or go online to our website at **http://www.yourtruenature.com** to order. Decide on how many trees you would like to order and for what occasions. If you use this order form, mail it to us with your enclosed check. (Note: Order for all your upcoming needs-cards do not expire)

2. We will mail you the number of tree planting kits (pictured above) you ordered. Each kit contains a postcard to mail to us and a greeting card and envelope to mail to the person or family you are planting the tree for.

3. You will receive your planting kit(s) within two weeks. Simply mail the completed postcard to us with the name and occasion you are planting for so we can plant the tree. Mail the personalized tree planting greeting card to the person(s) you are planting the tree for.

QTY ($8.95)	QTY ($18.95)	OCCASION
___	___	Birthday
___	___	Friendship
___	___	Memorial
___	___	Holiday
___	___	All Occasion
___	___	Birth
___	___	Anniversary
___	___	Wedding
___	___	Graduation
___	___	Congratulations
___	___	Fathers Day
___	___	Mothers Day
___	___	Thank You

Your Name _____
Address _____
City/State/Zip _____
Email _____
Telephone _____

Total Qty ____ at $ 8.95 = $ _____
Total Qty ____ at $18.95 = $ _____
CO residents add 2.9% sales tax $ _____
Shipping $ 3.75
GRAND TOTAL $ _____

Send with your check to: Your True Nature, Inc. Box 272309, Ft. Collins, CO 80527, (800)992-4769, Email us at: grow@yourtruenature.com.
Order online at **www.YourTrueNature.com**

A Thousand Things
Went Right Today!

They Went Right
Yesterday!

And They Will Go Right
Tomorrow!